# BE SMALL, FIGHT BIG

How Small Businesses Can Fight
Like a Fortune 500 and Win the
War on Talent

By

Benjamin J. Vezina, M.S

**This book is dedicated to:**

*My family. Without your support in all of my adventures, and misadventures, this book would not have been possible.*

# TABLE OF CONTENTS

# INTRODUCTION

Have you ever spent weeks interviewing and screening potential candidates only to find that when you finally made a decision, they accepted a job somewhere else? More importantly, have you lost candidates to a fortune 500 or larger corporations? Ever feel overwhelmed or that you simply can't compete for talent in this landscape? If you answered yes to any of the above, you are not alone.

Finding great talent can be an emotional rollercoaster ride and screening for talent is only one of the many hats that small business owners have to wear. Unfortunately for most small business owners, it is the hat they wear most often. To compound the pressure of wearing the hiring manager hat more times that we would like to admit is the fact that most small business owners don't have a background in candidate selection.

Hey, I get it. I have worn the "many hats" as well and you can't be an expert at all things, but candidate selection is not one of those things you can just fake it till you make it. You have to get good at it and get good at it fast. The success of your business depends on your ability to hire and retain great talent! If you are like most people; you're not 100% sure how to conduct a great interview, what to ask, what a good response really is nor how to make a sound decision based on said responses. Although we will discuss interviewing in this book, the secrets to finding great talent are more complex than simply asking questions and picking the best liar. There are a variety of constructs and challenges that are holding you back. Many that you aren't even aware of. No worries, we will expose the flaws in your hiring practices and will give you the tools that you need to make better hiring decisions.

In this book, you will learn how to modify the strategies of large corporations to win the war on talent. You will adapt and modify those strategies to fit the unique challenges of a small business owner. In doing so you will not only increase the quality of your hiring decisions, but also the speed at which you make said decisions. In essence, you will be small, but fight big.

# THE STORY BEHIND THE STORY

I wrote this book simply because of my own personal struggles and the missteps that I made when first starting out as an entrepreneur and small business owner. I wish I had a resource and a system that I could have used to make better hiring decisions. Unfortunately, no such system existed. Everything I could read on interviewing methodologies and making better hiring decisions seemed incomplete or geared towards larger organizations that had resources that I as a small business owner just didn't have. I created this system and wrote this book to help small business owners find better talent and build high performing teams. The methods in this book can be used by anyone who needs to hire great people, but I wrote it with the small business owner and their unique challenges in mind. I hope that it answers some questions for you and I know that it will give you a process for making better hiring decisions. The be small-fight big method has served me well and I am certain that it will do the same for you.

# CHAPTER ONE
## THE HAMSTER WHEEL OF DEATH

It was simple she thought to herself as the binder hit the wall. She would just have to work another double shift today. She didn't like the idea much nor did she really think it was simple, but she didn't have a choice. This was the fourth person in 3 weeks to quit without notice. Well, one she had to fire, but the result was the same. She would be working another open to close.

This was the 4th double shift in a week and she lost count of how many hours she had pulled over the last few months. She was a business owner she thought to herself. Wasn't it supposed to be glorious? Wasn't she supposed to be working less and making more?

"Ugggggg," Sara moaned as she slammed her fist down on the desk. "This is ridiculous," she mumbled under her breath.

Perhaps Mary could come in she thought? No, she couldn't redo the schedule again. What few employees she had left would quit as well. She had already asked them to change their plans too many times over the last few months. She would have to suck it up and work the shift.

She would stay late, finish the payroll and cut checks this evening. If she was lucky, she could get home by 11 she thought. Then she would get back here around 4 am tomorrow and get all the prep work for the day done. After that, she could start baking pastries and desserts. While the pastries are baking, she could start the opening procedures and get the dining area ready for guests. She would have to run the restaurant alone for a couple of hours playing double duty between server and cook, but she could make that work as long as they weren't too busy.

"Am I really wishing my business has a slow day?" she said with a grunt. Working alone and wishing for a slow day, how did it come to this? This unfortunately wouldn't be the end of her day. This was just the start. After Tim comes in maybe she could look at a few resumes and start the recruiting and onboarding cycle over, again.

She was spending too many hours reviewing resumes and conducting interviews only to hire someone who would eventually quit in a few weeks. Then, she would start the process all over again. Many never even stayed long enough to get a full grasp of the position. How many times had she recruited for the same position in the last

6 months? 4 or 5? She stopped counting a long time ago.

Reviewing resumes and working the extra shift wasn't what was really bothering her. What was really depressing her was the fact that she knew it would be another month at least before she had someone who could adequately fill the position. She would have to wear multiple hats and work several double shifts for at least that long all while training the new person. That was assuming she could find someone quickly.

She also would, of course, have to miss her son's recital tomorrow afternoon, but that was one of the sacrifices you make as a business owner, right? Surely, he would understand once he was older, she thought. Heck, one day when he's running this place, he will understand why she was always so absent. Then it occurred to her, did she really wish this frustration and stress on her children? No, this was not the kind of life she desired for her children nor did she want to pass a mountain of stress and frustration onto them. Something would have to change. She needed to get off this vicious cycle of long hours, constant recruiting and training, missing out on life, and then repeat.

And that's when she recalled something. She remembered a friend Morgan, who gave a talk at a chamber event last year about what he called the hamster wheel of death. If anything, that's what she felt like she was constantly living on. A wheel that keeps you running, but takes you nowhere.

How did Morgan do it so well? Not only did he seem to be doing well but he had multiple locations. Surely, he must be pulling his hair out and working 80 hours a week. Looking him up on social media she found that he had actually just got back from Barbados. What the heck she thought. No way, he must be putting on a facade. She knew a lot of business owners who pretended to be doing well but were really struggling just like her. They pretended all was well meanwhile the ship was burning down around them.

Sitting alone in her office, Sara began to cry. The dream of business ownership wasn't what she thought it would be. She thought she would be making more money, spending more time with her family, and having no one but herself to answer to, and that her stress and frustration levels would be nonexistent. "Boy was I wrong," she laughed a little through the tears.

But what if Morgan wasn't putting on a facade she thought. Maybe he really was onto something with his talk about the hamster wheel of death. Perhaps he could help her or perhaps he was really just full of it. She didn't really know but either way, she was going to find out. Wiping the tears away from her cheeks she picked up her phone and dialed Morgan's number.

# SUMMARY

The small business owner hamster wheel of death can take on many forms. It can be one thing or any number of things combined that keeps you running in circles but getting nowhere. The hamster wheel of death kills your business slowly and painfully while your stress levels reach critical mass. In this chapter, we touched on a few of the most common issues that keep small business owners on the hamster wheel of death.

They are:

1.  Constantly working IN your business instead of ON your business.
    A. You cannot be effective and grow your business if you are constantly having to work in your business 80% or more of the time.
    B. You already wear too many hats, you must reduce the number of hats you wear and more importantly the time spent wearing

them (trying to do everything yourself).

    C. When something springs a leak you have no wiggle room. You are the fallback plan, but you are already at max capacity.

2. Always recruiting

    A. Turnover is too high

    B. Poor selection processes and no time to improve them (you are already maxed out on time)

    C. You suck as a leader and/or you have a bad culture.

3. Always training or onboarding

    A. Because you have a high turnover ratio.

    B. You don't have any real training or onboarding programs in place.

    C. Sticking people in positions they aren't any good at or that they don't want to be in. We usually do this because we don't want to do said work ourselves. Maybe you aren't that good at "x" yourself? If you suck at marketing don't try to train someone else on marketing. Spend the money hiring a marketer. Contract out work that brings little value to your bottom line, but takes up a lot of your time.

The above list is by no means a complete list of the constructs that keep small business owners on the hamster wheel of death. They are simply the most common things that I have found keeping small business owners from being successful. As you can see most of the items above feed into one another and there are some overlaps. As we progress through this book, we will come back to several of the constructs above, but mostly we will address the core issue keeping you on the hamster wheel of death. We will address the one thing at the center of it all, the thing keeping most of us up at night, the ability to (or lack thereof) to hire great talent.

Small businesses are unique and their recruiting practices should be as well. However, there are a few strategies we can learn, or steal, from larger organizations to improve your ability to acquire great people. In the upcoming chapters, you will learn how to modify and apply the hiring tactics of the fortune 500 to give you an edge on recruiting the best and the brightest talent. Being a small business is not a disadvantage when it comes to winning the war on talent. If applied properly it can actually be your greatest asset. But before we can get you off the hamster wheel of death, we have to address the biggest obstacle that is keeping you on it, you.

# CHAPTER TWO
## BE SMALL, FIGHT BIG

**"**Morgan," Sara said, "thank you so much for taking time, to meet with me today."

"Anytime," Morgan said with a smile. "It's been too long since we had a chance to catch up. So, what's on your mind? You sounded upset the other day on the phone."

"I'll get to the point," Sara said with a stoic look on her face. "My business has been running me ragged. The business itself is doing pretty good, but I'm working myself to death." "And well," she paused for a moment, "I caught your talk last year about the hamster wheel of death and was wondering if you could give me some pointers?"

"Of course, I'll help you, but let me ask you this. The hamster wheel comes in many forms," Morgan said with a serious look. "What do you think is keeping you running, but getting nowhere?"

"Well, I seem to be spending most of my time either recruiting someone, training someone, or working a shift because someone just quit. It's a vicious cycle and I can't ever seem to get ahead."

Morgan nodded, "It's a tough cycle to break."

"Very," Sara said, "and I can't seem to find time to hire anyone because I'm spending all my free time covering shifts for those that just bailed on me, but you seem to make it look so simple. You have 3 locations and from what I can tell you are hardly ever at any of them. How do you do it?"

"Be small, fight big," he said with a wry smile.

"Be what to uh?" she asked with a confused look.

"Be small, fight big," Morgan repeated. "It's a system or a set of tactics that I use to help me stay off the hamster wheel when it comes to finding great talent."

"But what do you mean by," pausing for a moment she finished, "be small, fight big?"

"Large organizations have resources, tools, people, and money. A lot more money," he went on, "than we small businesses do. We simply can't win the war on talent spending all our hard-earned money on recruiting tools, right?"

Shifting her weight in the chair she nodded in agreement.

"Large corporations due to their resources and deeper pockets would always beat us out," Morgan said waving a finger in the air. "but we can't just give up. We must compete and win when we can, in the war for talent. Our businesses success depends on our ability to find great talent, our families depend on it, the families of the people we employ depend on it, and heck even the economy depends on it. Over half the nation is employed by a small business."

She could tell he was getting excited about this. She could tell by his gestures and the tone in his voice that he was clearly very passionate about whatever it was or wherever it was this conversation was going. So much so, that she thought better of interrupting him. So, she sat there in silence and let him go on.

"I'm rambling a bit, aren't I?" asked Morgan.

Sara smiled but didn't say anything.

"I'll give you the short version," Morgan said with a chuckle. "Years ago, when I first decided to leave corporate America and start my first small business, I was on the hamster wheel almost immediately. I was up all hours working myself to death and my stress levels were maxed out. What I was doing to find talent, and to train my talent, simply wasn't working. I came to realize that there truly is a war for talent, and if we are going to be successful, we had better start winning a few battles. Follow me?"

"Yes sir," Sara nodded.

"I knew I couldn't keep doing what I was doing with regard to finding talent. I also knew that I couldn't apply the tactics exactly as a fortune 500 size company," he exclaimed. "No, they have an entire HR team with hundreds of people to do the leg work that I simply didn't have access to. And that's when it hit me. Why couldn't I use some of the methods and tactics of larger corporations, but modify them to fit the unique situation and limited resources of a small business? And that's exactly what I did, be small because we are, but fight big as the larger corporations do."

"Ok," she said, "I think I get it. We are small, but we use the tactics of bigger or larger corporations to find the best talent. Albeit modified tactics to suit our particular needs; be small, fight big."

"You got it!" he exclaimed jumping from his chair and touching his finger to his nose.

"Ok, but is this something that you can teach me?" Sara asked excitedly.

"Yes, of course it is, but first you have to have the right mindset," Morgan explained. "These methods are worthless and ineffective if you do not have the right mindset when attempting to implement them. Not only will they not work, but you will find your hamster wheel is now starting to spin even faster."

"Oh, I definitely have the right mindset," said Sara. "I am so ready to get off this hamster wheel and start finding great talent."

Morgan shook his head slowly before locking eyes with Sara. "If wanting was enough we would all have everything our hearts desire," he said slowly. "No, you don't have the right mindset I'm afraid, but you will. Here is your first assignment on the 'Be Small, Fight Big' method. Go home tonight and write down 4 or 5 things that are keeping you from finding great talent. Come back here tomorrow and we will discuss them."

She thought about arguing the merits of her mindset. She knew she wanted off the hamster wheel and was confident that she was ready to learn the 'Be Small, Fight Big' method, but knowing Morgan the way she did it was unlikely he would be swayed. She would follow his direction and if it got her off the stress express sooner rather than later, what was another day?

"Deal," she said, "I'll see you in the morning."

# SUMMARY

Small businesses don't operate like larger corporations and small business owners don't work like typical leaders. In this chapter, we set the premise for what being small, but fighting big is all about. Fighting like a fortune 500 to win the war on talent, but doing so within the confines of our businesses. A few key concepts to keep in mind.

1. Most small business owners do not have a strategy or any tactics around acquiring top-level talent.
   - A. What's your methodology for finding great talent?
   - B. Is it teachable?
   - C. Have you had great luck duplicating it consistently?

2. Larger corporations have resources you simply do not.

A. Money and other resources for sourcing candidates at a level that you cannot compete and win at.

B. HR staff that can do all the heavy lifting and leg work. HR staff can prescreen candidates, place ads, conduct interviews, and other key recruiting functions. Being a small business owner, you more than likely have to do all of the above on your own (and the other duties required for you to keep your business running).

3. Be small, fight big.

A. Small businesses can use some of the tactics that larger corporations use to find and retain great talent.

B. Modifying those tactics to fit our unique challenges actually is an advantage, not a disadvantage (more to come on this in the following chapters).

Being small and fighting big is the solution to winning the war on talent, but there are other things also stopping you from finding great talent. This book would not be complete nor effective if we didn't address those issues first. Which is what we will do in the next chapter.

# CHAPTER THREE
## NO MORE EXCUSES

Sara was a little tired as she drove to Morgan's office the next day. She didn't sleep well as the excitement about learning the be small, fight big method keep spinning through her head most of the night. Prior to trying to sleep, she had spent a couple of hours creating her list of the top 5 things that were keeping her from finding great talent. She couldn't wait to review it with Morgan. She just knew that he would help her pick apart each of them and then she would get off the hamster wheel that was keeping her from growing her business.

Giving Morgan a brief hug as she entered his office she proclaimed, "I have completed the assignment you requested."

"Awesome," said Morgan as he extended his hand, "let's have a look at it."

As Morgan took the piece of paper and moved behind his desk Sara went on, "I can't wait to pick these obstacles apart. They really are the things that are keeping me from finding great talent."

"I'm sure they are," he said as he took his seat. Then sitting up straight he looked Sara in the eyes and crumpled the paper before saying, "these are total bullshit."

"Um, what?" Sara asked.

"Bullshit," Morgan repeated.

Sara with a confused look stuttered, "but no, those really are the top 5 things keeping me from finding great people."

"No, those are bullshit," Morgan said with a stern voice. Then with a slightly softer tone, he said, "Listen, I know that you believe they are and that's part of the problem. I apologize for having you go through that, but it was necessary. I knew yesterday when I gave you that assignment that it didn't matter what you wrote down. The list was going to be bullshit. Again, I apologize for having you go through it, but you needed to hear that and also what I'm about to say."

"Ok," Sara nodded.

"What you need to realize is that you and in particular that list of excuses is the biggest problem with your hiring process," Morgan went on. "No amount of tactics or money will help you find great talent if you have a list of fallback excuses."

"Fallback excuses? Sara asked.

"Yes, fallback excuses," Morgan answered. "We as humans will often create a list of 'what we believe to be reasons' to safeguard our feelings and ego in case we fail. These are unfortunately not really reasons, but just excuses. These excuses are often outside of our control and easy for us to pass the blame onto, thusly saving our ego the hurt. Take for example your first excuse."

"I cannot afford to pay what my competitors pay for great talent," she interrupted.

"Yes, total bullshit!" he exclaimed. "Research has proven time and time again that although the pay is a consideration, it is rarely the deciding factor of whether or not someone accepts a position. If that were so, we could simply offer more money to an employee that is quitting and they would then stay, right?"

Sara nodded, but before she could speak Morgan asked, "has that ever worked out for you?"

"No and the one time someone did stay because I offered more money, they just quit a few weeks later anyway," she said.

"See total bullshit, and you been using that excuse for how long?" making more of a statement than asking a question Morgan continued. "Let's take another one."

"Ok, what about how no one wants to work unless its full time?" she asked. Thinking she had him now. No way could he talk around this one. This was a legit reason for not being able to find great people.

"Now that could be a legitimate reason and not just

an excuse," he conceded.

Sara began to smile. She had him she thought. People only wanted fulltime work and not just part-time or temporary positions. This was a big issue for her as she really only needed a couple of part-time positions to be filled at the moment.

"But that's just bullshit as well," said Morgan with a smile. "I called David the owner of the restaurant across the street from you and he told me that about 80% of the people working for him are just part-time college students."

"Really?" Sara asked.

"Really," Morgan answered. "Now, I will agree that sometimes there are legit reasons for having an issue finding great talent. I usually give it this litmus test to determine if it's a reason or an excuse, but make no mistake it doesn't really matter."

"Why is that?" asked Sara.

"Because reason or excuse it doesn't change your situation. You must find great talent!" said Morgan with excitement. "Your business and your family depend on it. We make excuses to make us feel better about failing to find great people, and while we might feel better, we are still in the same situation. We are still on the hamster wheel and still not any closer to finding great people."

"Ok," Sara agreed, "but what's this litmus test?"

"It's actually very simple," Morgan said. "So much so that people often overlook it, but it's so crucial to checking yourself against bs excuses. I even had it printed and framed." Pointing to a print on the far wall. "Take a look."

Sara stood and moved to where the print was hanging. It was a simple white background with black lettering. It looked old and the simple wooden frame seemed out of place next to some of the nicer things in his office. Inside the wooden frame were 4 statements.

1. Are your competitors finding great talent?
2. Are other businesses in your community having the same struggle?
3. Remember, people want challenging and rewarding work with fair pay PERIOD.
4. Regardless if you answered yes or no to the above. Your business, your employees, their families, your family, your success, and even your community are counting on you to find great people. You have to find them anyway!

"So, are you competitors finding great talent?" he asked.

"Yes, of course, they are," she replied.

"And are other businesses in the community having the same hiring and high turnover problem that you are?" he asked.

"I imagine that some are, but most probably are not," she said shaking her head slightly.

"So, what does that tell you?"

She thought for a second. He was right. She was making excuses. Her direct competitors were finding great talent in this community. Her fellow business neighbors were not having the same problems that she was having. He certainly wasn't. No, the issue wasn't geography or the local talent pool. The problem was her.

"Bullshit," she said loudly, "it tells me my excuses are total bullshit and more importantly that I am part of the problem."

"Exactly," he said with a smile, "and if it's not an excuse, but ends up as a legitimate reason that's ok. A reason you can work around. Usually, you can find a solution to something that has a reason as its source, but excuses are the things we tell ourselves that often have no solution. They are the things outside of our control and make us feel better about our failure."

"Ok, but what about the last two items?" she asked.

"Those two things I added a few years ago to keep me grounded. Whenever I am struggling with finding talent,

I read that print and the last two remind me what people are really looking for. It's rarely money by the way. They can work anywhere for money and probably even more money than either of us can afford to pay. If money was all we worked for everyone would be a doctor or lawyer. No, everyone is not a doctor or lawyer because money is not the ultimate motivation when we decide to work or not work somewhere."

"Well, what is then?" Sara asked.

"It's different for everyone," Morgan replied. "Some people just want to get out of the house. Others might like some of the perks of working at a particular place or working there makes them feel good about themselves. That's why some people work for non-profits. It's not the money, it's almost always something else. You just have to pay a fair wage and find the 'it' of your business."

"That makes sense," Sara said with a look of realization. "I think I get the last statement."

"Yeah, that one keeps me honest," he said with a pause. "At the end of the day, you still have to find great people. Your business won't thrive without them. So, you have to put the BS aside and find them."

He could tell by looking at her that she was starting to get it. She was realizing that finding people was hard, but achievable if she got the excuses out of the way first. He smiled inwardly for a moment then said, "there's one last thing before we are done today. Follow me if you will," as he gestured towards the door.

Sara got up and followed him out of his office and into the employee breakroom. "Take a look at this," he said pointing to a print on the wall. The print was similarly framed just like the one in his office. On the print in the same simple black font was printed:

What sets you apart and makes you the "go-to" place everyone wants to work?

"This is a question you must ask yourself, Sara," Morgan said. "You must ask yourself today and as often as you can as your business continues to grow because the answer will change over the years. You must ask yourself, why would or should anyone want to work for me?"

Sara nodded as he could tell she was letting the statement sink in.

"Even more importantly ask yourself if you would work for you or your organization," Morgan chided. "Then ask yourself why that is or isn't. You might be surprised at how you answer that question knowing you have to support it. Everyone wants to automatically say yes, I would work for me, but having to explain it gives it substance. It might even motivate you to change a few things about your business or yourself."

"Yes, I see what you mean," Sara replied. "I'm a bit of a grump in the mornings. I don't think I would enjoy working for me till after lunch." They both laughed a bit before she continued, "but your right. I might want to look into changing that."

"You betcha," Morgan smiled, "but it's not just about removing behaviors. Answering those questions can help you come up with some things you might want to add to your business that makes you the 'go-to' place to work."

"Such as?" Sara asked.

"Well," Morgan paused before continuing, "for instance, maybe it's a great training program. Maybe they can bring their child to work or you have super flexible hours. Perhaps you have a reputation in your industry or community for developing great leaders and people want to work with you because of that. Yes, you might lose them after a couple of years, but it's a position that you didn't' have to fill for 2 years. That's way better than having to fill it several times a year. Talk about getting off the hamster wheel, right?"

"Yes," Sara replied with great enthusiasm, "but why do you have this phrase hanging here?"

"I actually have it hanging in several spots throughout

the facility and it's the same at all our locations," Morgan said. "And the answer is simple. Because hiring great talent and creating the 'go-to' place to work in your community is not just one person's job. It's everyone's job!" Morgan said with great enthusiasm. "Everyone that works here knows that hiring great people is part of what makes this company great. In keeping it at the forefront of everyone's mind, it keeps the 'go-to' answer at the top of our focus. So that we never lose that thing that makes us the 'go-to'. Does that make sense?"

"Yes, it does," she replied. "So, keeping it plastered everywhere makes sure that everyone remembers the 'go-to' reason for working here and they make sure they maintain whatever that reason is, correct?"

"Exactly," Morgan said. "When you discover your 'go-to' reason or reasons, make sure everyone knows what they are and that they must be maintained. They must also know that finding great talent is everyone's responsibility. Not just yours."

Wow, she thought to herself. Morgan had given her a lot to think about. Some of this stuff was simple, but for whatever reason, she had never considered it. She guessed she was just too focused on the symptoms of the hamster wheel instead of focusing on the source of the issue, herself.

"Morgan, you have given me a lot of things to consider

and you have given me a lot of questions that I must ask myself," she said with a serious look. "What else should I know before we can get into the first actual be small, fight big lesson?"

Morgan smiled that wry smile of his and said, "Sara, I actually have a confession to make. Having the right mindset is the first lesson in be small, fight big method. If I told you that upfront, today would not have been as productive. I am truly sorry, not sorry, that I had you conduct the exercise of creating a list of hiring obstacles and for what had to be said, but you needed to hear it."

"Yea, I sure did," she agreed.

"Awesome," Morgan said, "now you are ready for the next lesson. Tomorrow I want you to go see Heather in accounting. She will explain to you the next lesson. When you are done there come by and see me, ok?"

"Ok, see you then," She nodded and put the little notebook that she had been taking notes on back into her purse. As she reached her car in the parking lot, she wondered what new insights she would uncover tomorrow.

# SUMMARY

Often the biggest obstacle that is standing in the way of our success is us. This has been said often and applied in a variety of different ways, but when it comes to small business ownership and recruiting top talent it truly is the largest obstacle between you and your success. Just in life, so it is true in business, that we often create obstacles that don't truly exist. We make excuses for poor performance that cannot be refuted.

In this chapter, we discussed some of those excuses that make us feel like the problem is external and out of our control. We looked at some of the most common excuses or stories that we tell ourselves. We also expanded on some other concepts that keep us from finding great talent.

1.  We create external excuses that are beyond our control to make ourselves feel better about not finding great talent.

    A. There is a difference between the reason

and an excuse. Make sure you aren't just creating excuses.

B. It might make you feel better about your situation, but you are still in your situation.

C. Even if all that were true, find a way anyway. You still have to find great talent or your business is done. No business can operate without great people.

2. What sets you apart and makes you the "go-to" place everyone wants to work?

A. It's not always money. In fact, it rarely is the motivation for accepting a position or staying in it. What perks do you have that make you different from your competitors? (examples: in house child care, flexible hours, awesome retirement, discounts on product, etc.)

B. Do you have a reputation for developing great leaders or some other aspect that makes people want to work with you? If not, can you build that reputation?

C. Do you have challenges or unique situations that people find exciting? (examples: personal growth and leadership opportunities, opportunities to impact something personal to the individual)

3. If your neighbors can do it so can you.

    A. Are your competitors finding great talent? What are they doing that you are not? What sets them apart from you?

    B. Are other businesses in your community having the same struggle (high turnover or issues finding talent)? If not, the problem is not geography.

    C. People want challenging and rewarding work with fair pay. You don't have to offer the largest salaries to find great talent, just be in the ball park.

---

### Bonus Material

Get the Be Small, Fight Big companion workbook for free at:
Besmallfightbig.com

---

# CHAPTER FOUR
## YOU HAVE TO DIG DEEP

❝Heather, such a pleasure to meet you and I appreciate you making time for me today," Sara said as she walked into Heather's office.

"No problem at all," Heather said with a smile.

"So, what's today's lesson all about?" Sara asked.

"It's all about digging deep," Heather replied.

"Digging deep?" Sara asked with a puzzled look on her face.

"Yep," Heather said. "What we have to realize is that people are very complicated creatures and what we often see on the surface is only a fraction of who they truly are. What do you remember about fifth grade science?"

"A little I suppose. It's been a few years," she said laughing a little.

"Well, remember how the earth is made up of layers?" Heather asked. Waiting for Sara to nod she continued. "I want you to think of people like the earth and its layers." Heather then handed Sara a card with a photo of the earth and its layers printed on it. However, where the photo would normally say: crust, upper mantle, lower mantle, outer core, and inner core it was replaced with new descriptions. The new descriptions starting at the outer crust were: behavior, knowledge, attitudes, values, and personality & abilities.

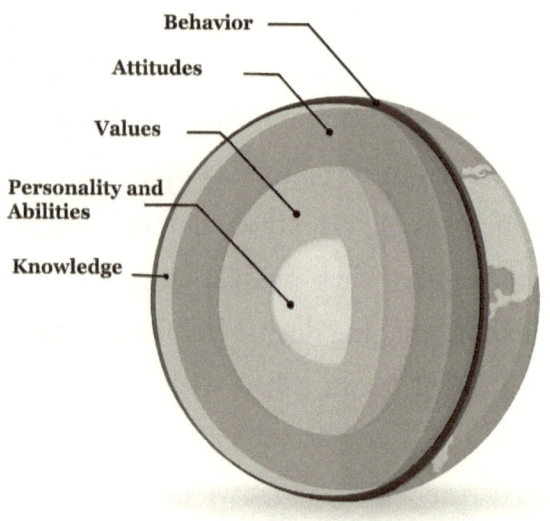

"Ok, but why is this important to hiring great talent?" Sara asked.

"Understanding people, and more importantly what makes one individual a better choice over another individual is at the core of making great hiring decisions," Heather replied. "Pun totally intended," she chuckled, "and improving your hiring decisions is the whole purpose of be small, fight big method.

"I definitely want to improve my hiring decisions,"

Sara said, "please go on."

"As I mentioned earlier people are complicated and have multiple layers that make up who they are. Unfortunately, most recruiters, hiring managers, and even small business owners use only surface level information to make their hiring decisions," Heather said. "They do this without fully realizing it and it's a very common hiring trap to fall into."

"Ok, can you give me an example of what you mean by basing a hiring decision on just surface level information?" Sara asked.

"Sure," Heather responded, "often we screen resumes to determine who to interview and who to pass on, right?" Heather paused a moment waiting for Sara to nod before continuing. "Sometimes we make an unconscious decision about that person without even meeting them based fully off of their resume. Screening resumes is not a bad thing. It is highly recommended, but we make unconscious decisions or create notions about those individuals based on the resume without ever even posing one question to that individual."

"Ok, I get what you mean," Sara said.

"To make the matter worse resumes are not always accurate. They are often exaggerated or 'spruced up'" Heather said making an air quotes gesture. "We then carry that bias or preconceived notion about that individual into the rest of the hiring process. We often tailor, without realizing it of course, our interview questions around that bias so that we can prove what we already believe about that person. That's why it is so important to conduct only structured interviews. They will make sure that you dig deep."

"Structured interview, what do you mean exactly?" asked Sara.

"Structured interviewing is a scientific process that greatly improves your ability to make better hiring decisions. Morgan will teach it to you in a later lesson. For now, let's just focus on the lesson of digging deep."

"Ok," said Sara pulling out her notebook and pen. She was excited to be learning about the complexities of what makes people different and how it applied to make better hiring decisions. She was also glad that Heather was taking such a complex topic and breaking it down into a simple to understand metaphor.

"Behavior is our outer level," Heather went on, "it's what we see on the surface, it's observable and gives some insights into the person, but we have to be careful. Behavior can be faked and above all, behavior changes depending on the situation. Ever notice how we might act one way around one group of friends, but then totally different around our coworkers or when say, our parents are present? Behavior is not a good indicator of how someone will perform in the future at work and when we are screening potential employees that is what we are doing. We are trying to make a guess or decision on how they will perform in the future if hired."

"I can understand that," Sara said scribbling into her notebook.

"The issue with behavior also carries over into the interview," Heather continued. "Most people will act one way during the interview while trying to get the job, but behave or perform differently once actually hired. Have you ever made a hiring decision and a few months later scratch your head thinking, what was I thinking when I hired this person?"

"Ummmm, yea, a few more times than I would like to admit," Sara laughed.

"That's because they fooled you in the interview. They behaved one way while being screened, then another once hired!" Heather exclaimed.

"I think I understand," said Sara. "Behavior alone is not a good indicator to base your hiring decisions on, correct?"

"Exactly," said Heather. "We are after the gold and you can only find gold by digging deep. We have to get into all those other layers if we are going to find gold, and to ultimately make a good hiring decision."

"Ok, so what's the next layer?" Sara asked as she gave

Heather her undivided attention.

"The next layer is knowledge," Heather went on. "What you are trying to uncover here is what do they know about the position or industry that will help them be successful should they get the job. The level of knowledge necessary will depend on the position."

Heather paused for a moment as she noticed Sara was taking notes, but also had a confused look on her face. "Don't worry, Morgan will teach you how to determine what items or constructs are important at each layer in a later lesson."

Sara smiled, "I was just thinking if someone really needed to know about baking or not to be able to work the cash register and things like that."

"Exactly," Heather said. "Now you are starting to get it. Not all knowledge about the business will be important. The only knowledge we care about is what is absolutely necessary for them to be productive in the position. The knowledge will become more or less important depending on the position in question. Morgan will teach you a process for sorting all that out and another process for how to uncover what they truly have inside them at a particular layer."

Sara nodded her understanding.

"Just like digging for real gold it's important to dig deep as we screen for potential employees, but it's also important to know where to dig," Heather said. "The deeper you go or the further you get away from those surface layers the more difficult it is for the potential candidate to deceive you as well.

"Ok," Sara said. "But what do you mean by knowing where to dig?"

Heather straightened in her chair. "If knowledge is not as important to the position, but say attitude is, then you want to dig more into the person's attitude and not so much into the knowledge of the individual. As I mentioned before, Morgan will show you a process for figuring out where to dig and another process for how to find out what someone has at that particular level. The key thing to remember right now is, that you have to dig deep if you want to find great talent. What is at the surface level, behavior, is often a bad indicator of future performance. Make sense?"

Sara nodded as she continued to take notes.

"In fact, I think I have shown you all I can about digging deep. Catch up with Morgan and he will get into the other layers with you and show you the next step in the be small fight, big system. Which is knowing where to dig," Heather said with a smile.

"Ok," replied Sara. "And I think you are correct. I haven't been digging deep enough. I usually make decisions on who to interview based on surface information in the resume.

Then I don't get deep enough when interviewing."

"Now you are getting it. We will have you fighting big before you know it," Heather said with a small wave as Sara left her office.

# SUMMARY

When selecting potential employees its best to think of the employee as being made up of much more than what's just on the surface. Don't take employees at face value, nor their resumes. If you want to find great talent and take your businesses performance to the next level you will have to dig deep. You will have to look beyond just the candidate's resume and their responses during the interview. Remember behavior can be faked and how someone acts in one situation doesn't necessarily mean they will act that way in other situations.

In this chapter, we discussed the multiple layers of an individual, at least the important ones when it comes to selecting the right candidate. Behavior is important, but knowledge, attitudes, values, skills, and abilities might be just as important depending on the job function. It's important to dig deep into each of those layers when selecting members of your team. To ignore any layer will keep you on the hamster wheel longer and stunt the growth of your business.

1. People are complicated, unique, and have multiple layers that make up the whole of their being.
    A. Think of the people like the layers of the earth.
    B. The layers from external to internal are: behavior, knowledge, attitudes, values, and personality and ability.
    C. All layers are important to us, but depending on the position some layers are more important than others.
2. Many small businesses use just the surface level to make decisions about hiring.
    A. Using just resumes and/or experience to make hiring decisions is a bad idea.
    B. Using just behavior is also a bad idea when making a hiring decision.
    C. People change behavior depending on the situation. They may act one way during an interview and very differently once on the job.
3. You have to dig deep to get to the gold.
    A. Digging deep is not easy, but worth the effort.
    B. The deeper you go the more likely you will find what you are looking for with

regard to determining potential future performance.

C. The deeper you go the more difficult it is for potential candidates to deceive you.

# CHAPTER FIVE
## KNOWING WHERE TO DIG

**M**organ was on the phone as Sara made it to his office. He waved her in and motioned for her to sit down as he hung up the receiver. Sara pulled out her note pad and pen ready to take notes. She was excited to hear more about the be small fight, big system. Getting off the hamster wheel was beginning to seem like a reality if she could hire some great talent.

"So, did you learn about digging deep?" asked Morgan.

"Yes, Heather was very helpful and I gained a lot of insights about what I was doing wrong from our short time together," said Sara. "I never thought about how a person or potential new hire needed to be looked at beyond just the surface level. I never thought about how sometimes what's at the core of a person can be more useful to us when making hiring decisions. I always just looked at their past and possibly their responses during an interview."

"Indeed, people are complex," said Morgan. "but

getting to the core of them, pun intended, is extremely important if we are to make good hiring decisions. Which leads us to our next lesson, knowing where to dig."

"Ok, but why is that important?" Sara asked with a serious look. "Can't we just dig deep, uncover who they really are and make a decision from there?"

"You could," said Morgan. "And you would be better off than not digging deep, but knowing where to dig will help you make an even better hiring decision. Think of it as if you are looking for gold. You wouldn't go digging for silver or another ore, would you? No, you are looking for gold, not silver. You could waste a lot of money digging in one place looking for something that is not there and perhaps the methods you would use looking for one type of ore over another would be inappropriate and costly. When you know where to dig you have a better chance of finding it and you might even save a little money in the process. Make sense?"

"Actually, it does," said Sara with a nod. "When you explain it that way it makes sense, but how do you know where to dig?"

"And that my dear is at the heart of the lesson," Morgan said with a wry smile. "Before you can know where to dig you have to know what is it that you are digging for. You have to know exactly what kind of employee you are looking for and what it is that you exactly want them to achieve or do," emphasizing the word exactly as he spoke.

Sara nodded her understanding.

"You are constantly having to hire, train, replace, and start over again for your front counter help and entry-level baker positions, correct?" Morgan asked.

"Yes, that's correct. It seems every couple of months I am having to refill those positions. It is no doubt one of the many things that keeps me on the hamster wheel and keeps me from growing my business," Sara replied.

"So, tell me," said Morgan as he leaned forward and cocked an eyebrow. "What criteria or job description are you using when hiring for those positions?"

"Well," Sara paused for a moment and used the back of her pen to scratch her head before continuing. "I suppose, criteria wise I'm just looking for someone: trustworthy, reliable, honest, and that has a good personality."

"And those are all admirable qualities," said Morgan. "However, they are a little vague, and that herein lies the problem with most job descriptions. Most hiring managers or small business owners use vague terms when looking for where to dig. They sometimes use descriptions that they found on the internet or that they simply wish for. Unfortunately, wishing and hoping is not a great plan when it comes to finding great talent. Besides, the things you mentioned should be a minimum standard to work for you, right?"

"Absolutely!" exclaimed Sara.

"So, this is one of the things that I learned working for a fortune 500 and I adapted it to work for the be small fight, big system," said Morgan. "It truly is the most important part. Knowing where to dig and what exactly you are looking for is the foundation for the rest of the entire be small fight, big system. So, here is your homework."

Sara repositioned herself in the chair and began taking notes feverishly.

"I want you to create a list of all the key performance indicators, also known as KPI's, for each position that you hire for," said Morgan. "Each position should have a different list of KPI's as each position has different responsibilities. Yes, there might be some overlap, but for the most part, they should look different. What your front counter worker produces or does for your business is not the same as your bakery staff or your accountant, correct?"

"No, certainly not," said Sara.

"And therefore, the KPI's should be very different as well. It's important to write these all down. This is a very important exercise Sara," said Morgan. "The list of KPI's can be as long as you want it to be, but at a minimum, you should have at least five to ten items. It's important that these items be something you can measure or observe."

"Ok," said Sara looking up from her notepad. "But what do you mean by measure?"

"Think of it as, what does success look like for this position," said Morgan. "For instance, one KPI for your bakers could be; the baker preps the store and creates 100 units in the first hour and 200 units per hour for the following 3 hours. You understand that prep takes time and the ovens have to warm, so the productivity is less the first hour. You see this is measurable, it has a number. You can easily tell if the individual is being successful or not."

Sara nodded, "but what about employees that don't produce a product like my front counter employees?"

"It's always better to have a number in most situations, but it's not a hard and fast rule," said Morgan. "You can use visual observation when applicable, but I bet if you really put your mind to it you could find something numerical to measure. For example, what is it that makes one front counter person more effective over another?"

"Oh, that's easy," said Sara. "Their ability to get customers in and out quickly. Most people are on their way to work in the morning and don't want to spend a lot of time in the store waiting. I have even seen people leave due to the wait."

"Ok, so one KPI might be the ability to take orders and fill those orders in under one minute," said Morgan.

"Or something like that, right?"

"Yes," said Sara with an excited look on her face.

"Another benefit of KPI's is that you can use them as the criteria for your performance reviews," said Morgan. "You will also use them to grow your business."

Sara looked up with a slightly puzzled expression on her face.

"When business performance is not where it should be," said Morgan. "You come back to your KPI's and figure out who or which departments aren't hitting them. From there you decide if is it time to have conversations or create new KPI's. As your business grows your KPI's will change occasionally, but the biggest benefit of clear KPI's is an easy way to determine if your employees are meeting the standards for success or not. Usually when a business is struggling it is because one or more employees are not meeting the KPI's for their position."

"That makes sense," said Sara.

"Once you have your list of unique KPI's for each position I want you to create a task list for each KPI," said Morgan. "Again, write it down. The tasks that you write down are the things that are required for someone to achieve or complete the successful outcome of the KPI. The tasks should be an action verb of some sort. For instance, for your bakers to achieve the outcome of 200 units an hour they will need to be able to: operate a mixing machine, measure raw materials, place mixed material onto a baking sheet, and apply glazes using the appropriate tools."

Sara nodded, "go on."

"The key thing to remember when creating the task list is it needs to be an action verb," said Morgan. "Some task lists for some KPI's will be longer than others. And one other thing I forgot to mention. When creating your KPI's and your task lists make sure to involve other members of your staff. You will be surprised at the things they know about the positions that you might simply overlook or dismiss."

"Ok, that makes sense," said Sara. "I also imagine that involving them will get them to start to understand that hiring great talent is everyone's responsibility."

"Absolutely," said Morgan with a huge grin. "The more you involve your team the more enthusiastic they will be about helping you find great talent. This will also get you off the hamster wheel quicker."

"I so badly want off this stress machine called the hamster wheel," said Sara with a chuckle.

"And you will get there," said Morgan. "Now before we go on to the last portion of knowing where to dig, do you have any questions?"

"No, I think I got it so far," replied Sara.

"Good," said Morgan. "So far you have two lists for

each position that you are wanting to find talent for. A list of KPI's which are measurable outcomes that define success for that position. You will have multiple KPI's for each position. The other list is a list of action tasks that the individual must perform if they wish to achieve the KPI. Make sense?"

"Yep," said Sara with a confident look on her face.

"There is one more list you will need to create to go with the other two and it's also just as important," said Morgan. "Remember your lesson on digging deep and how you were taught to think of people as existing in multiple layers like the earth's crust?"

Sara nodded.

"Our behaviors, the outer layer, can be thought of as the tasks for the most part," said Morgan. "For this exercise, the other layers will be our main focus. You will use the task list and ask yourself this question. What knowledge, skills, abilities, attitudes, values, and aspects of the person's personality are important to the completion of the tasks?

"Ah," said Sara as she let out a quick exhale. "This is what you mean when you say knowing where to dig."

"Exactly," said Morgan. "You need to know which skills and abilities, knowledge, values etcetera are important and which ones are not. And you need to know specifically. This is how you dig deep and how you know where to dig. If you get this part right finding great talent will be a cinch."

"Ok, makes sense, but how do I tie it all together," said Sara.

"Good question," said Morgan. "First thing though, if the tasks are similar and require similar KSA's you can group them together, but for the most part, I want you to create a grid for each task. At the top of the grid write the task and below it create a separate column for: knowledge, skills, abilities, values, and other."

"Got it," said Sara.

"Then you have to ask yourself and maybe some of the people on your staff, what does this person need to know to be successful?" said Morgan. "For example, your baker needs to know how to operate the oven, take accurate measurements, know the difference between how to measure liquids and dry goods. That's the knowledge layer and you would write those things down under that column. Keep in mind that you might have only a few things or an exhaustive list for each layer. You would do this for each column or layer creating a list of things at that particular layer that the potential new hire would need to know or exemplify in order to be successful on that particular task. Make sense?"

"Yes, it does," said Sara. "But this is going to be a lot of work."

"Yes, it will be," said Morgan. "but well worth it. It's going to massively improve your ability to make great hiring decisions as well as accelerate your businesses performance. It will also."

Sara cut him off completing the sentence, "get me off the hamster wheel!"

"You got it!" Morgan nodded with a smile. "One last thing. After you have each layer or column complete with a bullet point or two under each, I want you to underline everything that the potential new hire must be able to do or know on day one. If it's not a crucial aspect on day one or it's something that you can teach them quickly do not underline it."

"I can do that," said Sara.

"One more thing I should clarify, sometimes a layer or KSA will not have anything to do with a particular task. In those instances, leave it blank and let your common sense prevail. Make sense?" asked Morgan.

Sara nodded as she continued to take notes.

"Ok, I think that I have given you enough homework for today," said Morgan. "Take a few days and get with your team on this. It's a lot of work, but it's also very important to your success. Once you have your 3 lists created: KPI's, tasks, and layers grid come back and see me at the end of the week and I'll show you how to turn it all into gold."

Sara was grinning from ear to ear as she left Morgan's office. She could already see where this exercise and the data it produced was going to help her make better hiring decisions. She was ready to start fighting big and finding better talent for her team, and above all, she was ready to stop working so many doubles.

# SUMMARY

Knowing what you are looking for or where to dig, is the first step in finding what you are looking for. Too often business owners use generic job descriptions hoping that it helps them find a specifically talented individual. You have to get serious about what your business needs when it comes to talent and the skills that talent brings to bare for you and your organization. Remember, that hoping and wishing is not a strategy.

In this chapter, we discussed the processes that will help you uncover exactly what it is that you are looking for. We discussed the importance of key performance indicators and the tasks associated with achieving said KPI's. We then looked at the various layers that you must dig into to determine which knowledge, skills, and abilities employees must possess to be successful in the new position.

1. Know exactly what you are looking for.

   A. Don't rely on generic job descriptions. They will fail you and cause you to make poor hiring choices. Be very specific.

   B. Be very clear on your needs and expectations for this position. Write your expectations down. Involve others that might have valuable input about this position.

   C. What key performance indicators determine success in this position? Make sure they are measurable and observable when applicable.

2. Know exactly what tasks matter most to achieve success in this position.

   A. Create an extensive list of all the tasks that are required for this position.

   B. Every task on this list should be associated with a KPI. If it is not, then why are you having the new hire complete said task?

   C. Tasks should be an action verb in most situations. The employee should be able to count money accurately or the employee should be able to lift 50lbs of flour are good examples of a task.

3. What knowledge, skills, abilities, and other attributes help employees complete the tasks?

  A. What does the new hire need to know to be successful in completing the tasks?

  B. What skills, abilities, and other attributes do they need to be able to perform to be successful in this position? Will they need to be able to type 80 words a minute? Will they need to be able to design spreadsheets or marketing materials using a specific program?

  C. Do they need to know this knowledge and/or be able to perform the ability on day one or can you get them up to speed quickly? Sort crucial day one KSA's into a special pile as this will help you later in the selection process.

---

### Bonus Material

If you have not already downloaded the free
Be Small, Fight Big companion
workbook do so now. It has some great
examples of the various tools mentioned in
this chapter.
Do so at: Besmallfightbig.com

---

# CHAPTER SIX
## HOW TO DIG

Sara looked a little weathered as she entered Morgan's office on Friday morning. She had worked 2 doubles and over 30 hours in just the last couple of days. She was ready now more than ever to get off the hamster wheel and to start building a great team. Even though she was tired she was excited about today's lesson and had her trusty notepad at the ready.

"Long week uh?" asked Morgan.

"You could definitely say that," replied Sara.

"Well today's lesson is going to be a little more fun than the last couple because today we teach you how to dig," said Morgan.

"How to dig?" asked Sara with a puzzled look on her face.

"Yes, how to dig," said Morgan. "Today we tie together the previous lessons of digging deep and knowing where to dig and show you how to create a structured interview. The structured interview is where you truly start digging into all those KSA's and tasks that will help you make better and quicker hiring decisions as well as give you the ability to understand what makes one candidate a better choice over another."

"That sounds spectacular," said Sara. "Where do we begin?"

"We begin with the tasks sheets and the grid homework I had you do," said Morgan. "Do you have them completed for one of the positions you hire most often for?"

"I sure do," said Sara with a big smile as she handed Morgan a thick manilla envelope.

Morgan took the file and quickly sorted through the various lists. She indeed created lists for the KPI's, lists for the tasks necessary to achieve the KPI's, and the grids that broke down the various layers for each task.

"Great work," said Morgan. "I see you broke each task down into what layers or what: knowledge, attitudes, values, and personality and abilities are necessary to complete the task. Good work. We will call the layers KSA's for now, ok?"

"Totally," said Sara.

"And did you find the work daunting?" asked Morgan.

"Not as much as I thought it would be," said Sara. "And I must admit doing them in the correct order made a big difference. It made the process easier and I was able to get really clear on what KSA's are important for job success and which ones aren't. As opposed to the old way I was doing it. Which I hate to admit was kind of just guessing or being vague at best."

"Exactly, it's important to determine your KPI's, then your tasks, then your KSA's," said Morgan. "Doing it any other way doesn't create the clarity and focus you need to create a great structured interview."

Sara nodded her understanding.

"So, the first thing you want to do is pick the top six or so KSA's that correlate to job success or achieving your key performance indicators," said Morgan.

"Why only six?" asked Sara. "Why not all of them?"

"It's simple," said Morgan with a sheepish grin. "The be small fight, big system is all about making better hiring decisions. Doing so quickly and more efficiently. If we tried to dig up all of the KSA's we would be conducting three-hour interviews. We simply don't have the time nor the resources do to that. And besides, you will find that some KSA's are more important to success than others. I want to hire the person who is the best at the important KSA's, not the person who is good at the not so important ones. Make sense?"

"Actually, it does," said Sara. "Not sure why I never thought of it that way before."

"Don't beat yourself up over it," said Morgan. "It's actually very common. Most business owners and even some seasoned hiring managers make the same mistake of getting caught up on the small things, over the more important ones that truly drive our businesses success. This is why we focus our structured interview around the top 6 KSA's."

Sara nodded, "go on."

"Ok, now that you have your top 6 or so KSA's we need to define them," said Morgan. "Why we are doing this will make sense in a minute. You can create your own definition or use one you look up online. The how doesn't matter. What is important is that you have an accurate definition. For instance, you have problem-solving as a key ability for your front counter help. How would you define that?"

Sara pulled out her phone and looked up the definition online. "The web says it's the process or act of finding a solution to a problem."

"Ok, now that you have a definition you want to create a question that uncovers the KSA of problem-solving while keeping in mind the definition," said Morgan. "There are two basic types of questions that you want to create for uncovering KSA's and you can ask as many questions as necessary but if the question doesn't uncover a KSA directly then throw it out. The two types of questions are experiential and situational."

"Experiential questions focus on the past and

things the potential new hire has done previously. While situational questions focus on the future and hypothetical situations that the new hire might face while in the new position. Think of these as 'what if' scenario type questions," said Morgan. "There is a third type of question we need to consider called probing questions, but we will get into those in a minute. This all making sense so far?"

"Yes sir," mumbled Sara as she feverishly took notes.

"So, an experiential question for problem solving might look something like this," said Morgan. "Tell me about a time when you had to deal with a serious problem at work. What was the situation? Who was involved? What actions did you take to resolve the problem?"

"That's a really good question," said Sara.

"Thank you," said Morgan. "I just made it up on the fly. You are going to want to spend a little more time on it, but you get the gist of where I'm going with it. The key is to create questions that uncover and rate the person's ability for that particular KSA. If it doesn't do that, rework the question or throw it out. This is a good time to point out what a structured interview truly is."

"K," said Sara. "What is it?"

"An interview is an assessment just like any other," said Morgan. "You are making a decision based on that assessment and often comparing one potential candidate against another based on the data you glean from the assessment or interview. This is why it is super important for your interview to have a consistent structure, hence the name structured interview, so that it can give you consistent and reliable results. Meaning you ask all the questions the same way, in the same order, every single time you conduct an interview. Never omit or skip questions, even if you think you already know the answer or how they will respond."

"But why is that so important?" asked Sara.

"You want to compare apples to apples," said Morgan. "If you give one person one assessment and another person a different assessment, even though they might seem similar, you are actually comparing apples to oranges. That unfortunately is not going to help you make accurate hiring decisions, and accurate decisions is the key to making better candidate selections when you are trying to build a high performing team".

"That makes sense," said Sara. "So, then what?"

"Next you have to create a way to rate the potential candidates' responses," said Morgan tilting his head forward. "So far you have determined what KSA's you want to uncover. You have defined the KSA and created a question that will help you uncover the KSA. Now you create a rating scale."

"The first thing is to decide how many levels you will

have in your scale," said Morgan. "You want no less than three, but I always try for at least 5. Each question will use the same amount of levels. For each level, you will create a label and brief descriptor. The label can be as simple as good, better, best. I usually use novice, moderate skill, skilled, proficiently skilled, expert. Novice being a 1 and expert being a rating of 5. This make sense?"

"Yes," replied Sara. "But what about the descriptor?"

"Each descriptor will be specific to the KSA you are uncovering," said Morgan. "It might be something like, uses the skill exceptionally in difficult situations. Serves as a resource and helps others in similar situations. That would be for a level five rating. A level four might be, uses the skill in considerably difficult situations. Rarely needs assistance from others. Do you see the slight difference between the two?"

"Yes, I do," said Sara. "but how do I determine if someone's a four or a five?"

"Good question," said Morgan. "You will create, and I would use my team to help with this one, but you will create behavioral examples for each rating. Nothing too long, just a few bullet points for each level. This will serve you as a guide when trying to determine where to rate a candidate's response. Keep in mind that it's only a general guide and not an absolute as everyone's experiences will be different."

"Whoa, you got my head spinning Morgan," said Sara putting a hand to her head.

Morgan let out a little chuckle before continuing. "How about we create a little sample rating form to help get you started?"

Sara nodded, "that would definitely help."

Morgan opened his laptop and created a document. "Across the top, I put the KSA I'm trying to uncover. In a box below that, I put the question that I am going to ask. Below all of that, I will create a grid that has the rating levels down the left side. For this example, let's just use three. Novice will be our lowest rating, then skilled, then expert. Next to that, I will put the corresponding descriptor. Then in a box to the right of the descriptor, I will put our examples. I usually put one question to a sheet of paper, but if its small like this one I might squeeze two to a piece of paper. Off to the side, I will put my already determined probing questions."

"You mentioned probing questions earlier," said Sara.

"One sec and I'll get to that," said Morgan as he took the document off the printer and handed it to Sara.

Tell me about a time that you had to work with a coworker that you did not like. What was the situation and how did you resolve it, if it was resolved?

| Proficiency level | General Competencies | Behavioral/ Other Competencies | Probing Questions |
|---|---|---|---|
| Expert | Exemplifies the competency in extremely difficult situations. | Demonstrates expert understanding of the construct and is a resource to others. | What resources did you use to resolve the conflict? |
| Skilled | Exemplifies the competency in moderately difficult situations. | Demonstrates some understanding of the construct. Requires occasional guidance. | What other individuals did you involve or seek guidance from? |
| Novice | Exemplifies the competency in the most basic of situations. | Demonstrates awareness of the construct. Requires close supervision and guidance. | |

"Ah this makes more sense now," said Sara looking at the document. "I think I was overthinking it."

"No worries," said Morgan. "Now the key thing to keep in mind is to take lots of notes when conducting the interview. Don't worry about rating the person right then. You can if you prefer, but it's not crucial. I take lots of notes and keep the guide handy as a reference. Then once the person has left, I rate them. I then transfer all the rating to a rating form. The rating form can be a simple grid with each KSA in one box and the score in another box with a total at the bottom. The key is to rate them immediately. Do not wait as we tend to forget things or we get confused later in the day about who said what, when we are doing multiple interviews back to back. Make sense?"

"Totally," she replied.

"Now about probing questions," said Morgan. "Probing questions are just that. They probe a little deeper and clarify a response. You want to create a short list of probing questions for each interview question. You will only use those questions with candidates to ensure that you are being fair with each potential new hire. Keep in mind you won't always use probing questions. You will only use them if someone's response is vague or unclear. If someone's response is clear, you simply won't ask any probing questions, but when you do ask probing questions its always one already on your list. It might be something like, what led to the situation? Or something like, what resources did you use to resolve this?"

"Ok, that makes sense," said Sara.

"Good," said Morgan. "I know it seems like a lot, but I promise you after you have done a form for a couple of questions you will see that it's not that difficult. Also keep in mind, that after you have done a few interviews revisit this part of the process. You might need to change your questions up or create new examples for the various rating levels. The more you do this the more proficient you will become at it and also at knowing what good looks like. The key thing to remember is that whatever changes are made to the process when you begin another round of interviews all candidates go through the same process exactly."

"Hence the structure part of a structured interview," smiled Sara.

"You said it," chided Morgan. "Now get out of here. I have a tee time this afternoon. Catch up with me Monday and I'll share with you the last few pointers for fighting big."

"Sounds like a plan," said Sara as she gathered her things and headed out of Morgan's office.

# SUMMARY

Knowing how to dig is just as important as knowing where to dig and digging deep. The structured interview and knowing which KSA's drive business performance is the key to making better hiring decisions. Asking generic or random questions will never net you top-quality talent. Creating a reliable system or method of rating and comparing potential new hires not only speeds up the process but gives you the confidence to make better decisions.

In this chapter, we discussed how to create and implement a structured interview. We talked about how to define your KSA's and create powerful questions that will help you uncover if the potential candidate has the skills necessary to help your organization succeed. We created a process for rating and ranking your candidate's responses that will enable you to make better hiring decisions.

1. Determine which competencies or KSA's are important and which ones are not.

    A. Usually, choose only the top six or so KSA's to evaluate during the interview. Choosing more only waters down the effectiveness of your selection process. It's better to have a B level player in the crucial competencies for job performance over an A player on something that's only moderately important to success, in most cases.

    B. Create or define the KSA. A good definition of the competency is important to developing good questions and creating an accurate rating scale.

2. Develop the questions.

    A. You can use a mixture of experiential and situational questions where applicable or all of one type of question if you see fit. The questions should uncover at least one or more of the KSA's.

    B. Experience questions focus on the past. You would ask questions about how they handled or performed when "X" happened in a previous situation.

C. Situational questions look to the future. Think in terms of "what if or what would you do if this happens" types of questions.

D. A third type of question to consider are probing questions. These are approved follow up questions and it's important to know which ones you will ask. Don't go off script. It's important to ask the same questions to all candidates to ensure you are being fair with them and using a standardized method for rating and ranking your potential new hires. Probe questions are asked just like the regular interview questions in a specific and consistent way, but with one exception. You might not always ask probing questions to all potential hires depending on their response to the initial question, but when you do ask them you ask the same ones to all candidates. You wouldn't ask one candidate one set of probing questions and then use another set of questions for a different candidate. Think of these as standard follow up questions.

3. Create a rating system.

    A. Decide on the proficiency level. No less than 3, but 5 is probably best.

    B. Create a description or definition for each level.

    C. Create or determine what an appropriate response should look like for each proficiency level (a behavioral example).

    D. When conducting the interview take lots of notes. Make sure to complete the rating form immediately after the interview is finished and before moving onto other interviews.

# CHAPTER SEVEN
## FINDING A NEW BOX

66 How was your weekend?" asked Sara as she came into Morgan's office.

"It was great. Thank you for asking," said Morgan.

"So, what's the lesson for today?" asked Sara.

"This one is simple," he said. "I call it finding a new box."

"Finding a new box," Sara said with a confused look on her face. "Don't you mean thinking outside the box?"

"No, thinking outside the box is kind of played out," said Morgan. "So, we call this one finding a new box and its aptly named. In this lesson we want you to put a few new tactics into your box of hiring tools. These are things that most people simply never consider when looking for great talent, but they are very effective methods."

"Ok," she said with a nod as she got her notepad and pen out.

"There are three basic concepts to consider when finding our new box," he said. "First think about creating a unique situation. Second, stealing employees and third sharing employees. You can use all of these, one of these or none of these. They should be used when appropriate, but I implore you to think hard on each and consider where one or more of these methods might benefit you. Don't dismiss them out of hand."

"Ok, I won't," Sara said as she adjusted herself in the chair. "But what do you mean by creating a unique situation?"

"Take a look at the demographics of your area," Morgan explained. "Look at the usual stuff: age, gender, etc., but also think about socioeconomic information as well as education. For instance, we have a college nearby. That college is full of young adults that would love part-time work. Have you ever considered hiring any of them?"

"Not really," replied Sara. "Most of them can't work when I need them due to their school schedules."

"What's stopping you from modifying your needs or your schedule to accommodate them?" asked Morgan. "I'm not talking major overhauls, but slight tweaks."

"Nothing I suppose," she replied. "I guess I just never thought about it."

"And this is what I mean by creating a unique situation," smiled Morgan. "Create a unique position or restructure an existing one to fit with the demographic in your area. The same could go for a retirement community.

Many don't want to hire retired individuals because they don't think they are career-minded, and they probably aren't. However, you have people with an extremely open schedule and a lifetime of experiences that can be put to good use for your business."

"Wow," Sara exclaimed clearly excited at what Morgan just said. "I guess I never really thought about it. That gives me some ideas."

"Good, that's the point of finding a new box. Creating new ideas," Morgan said making a gesture with his hands as if he was grabbing onto an invisible box. "The thing to keep in mind about finding talent is not to get stuck on one type of person. Don't just look for single mothers or adults with no children because you think they will have a better schedule. Don't just hire adults with children because you think them more reliable and have a need to work. And above all, don't think outside the box. Create a new box for the people in your surrounding community, where applicable."

"That actually makes perfect sense," said Sara. "I have been pigeonholing myself on talent by trying to hire only one type of person, when there is a whole plethora of talent out there. I just need to create a unique situation for them to fit into."

Morgan simply smiled and tapped his finger to his nose.

"Ok, but what about the other two tactics?" asked Sara.

"Stealing talent is the oldest trick in the book for larger organizations," said Morgan. "But a word of caution. If they jumped to your ship easily, they will probably jump to another just as easily. Also, stealing employees is usually more expensive from a salary stand point. I steal employees from time to time, but I'm very selective in my decision and I'm very clear on why I want them in the first place."

Sara nodded as she continued to take notes.

"I can't state this enough," Morgan went on. "Be very clear about why you are hiring them. Do they have special knowledge or skills that are of value to your organization? Are they a temporary fix to get you through a particular problem and they have the unique skillset to fix your problem? If not, then stealing might not be the best option. Make sense?"

"Yes, it actually does," she replied.

"For example, I once stole an employee to get me through an expansion I was conducting. They were expensive, but had experience in my particular challenge. I knew they weren't going to stick around forever, but I didn't need them to. I just needed their help with the expansion. It worked out perfectly for us both," said Morgan.

"They filled a unique void in your current staff or helped you overcome a challenge that they were uniquely qualified for," said Sara. "But how do I steal an employee?"

"Each situation is different," replied Morgan. "The key is going back to lesson three, no more excuses. If you want to attract top-level talent without breaking the bank, then you must have something that makes you appealing to come work for. Is it flexible schedules for better work-life balance or maybe some remote work? Are you known for developing great leaders? If you are just like the place they are leaving, what's the point of jumping ship?"

Sara put her pen to her lips clearly in deep thought then nodded.

"I think you get the idea," said Morgan. "The last tactic in finding a new box is sharing employees. This is one of my favorite and it's often overlooked by small business owners. You would be surprised at how many people there are in this community that want to work more hours, but can't seem to find a position that will work with them. This tactic is great for temp and seasonal help, but also can be used for part-time and full-time positions."

"You already know what I'm going to ask," said Sara.

"How do I find employees to share?" Morgan asked with a smile.

"Yep," she chided back.

"It's actually easier than you think," he said. "I usually start with my powerbase or my network. I ask friends and family if they know of anyone looking for more work. Even if they already have another job. Everyone almost always knows at least one person looking for more work. They might not end up being a fit for what you're looking for, but you won't know till you ask."

"You know, I never really thought about that," said Sara. "I usually only ask if they know anyone out of work etc."

"Yes, and that's not a bad question to ask either," he went on. "But changing the question changes the referrals they will give you."

Sara nodded as she continued to take notes.

"The last thing to consider is simply asking your business neighbors," said Morgan. "You would be surprised at how many people are just on the other side of a shared wall that would love to come work for you. They are probably thinking like you're thinking, being closed-minded, and assuming you won't hire someone with another job or that your schedules won't collide. Your business neighbor might also be afraid they will lose an employee because they themselves can't give them enough hours. By referring and sharing them with you, they get to keep the employee and the employee gets the hours they need. It's a win-win for everyone when done right."

"You know what? I know both my business neighbors," said Sara. "And as you said we even share a wall, but I never thought to ask them about sharing employees."

"Most people don't," said Morgan. "Finding a new box means thinking about your business in new ways and I can't say it enough, don't dismiss these tactics lightly. As I have already warned, put some serious thought into these tactics. How can you create a unique situation for the demographic in your community? Can you steal or maybe share some employees to create win-win situations for all involved?"

"This lesson of finding a new box has given me a lot of things to consider," said Sara touching her pen to her temple.

"It often does," said Morgan. "And that my dear, is the final lesson in the be small fight, big system. If you implement each lesson in its entirety, you will be well on your way to getting off that hamster wheel."

"I will implement each lesson and I will get off that hamster wheel," said Sara clenching her fist. "Morgan, I can't say how much I appreciate you for teaching me these lessons. Can we stay in touch?"

"You are most welcome," Morgan said with a smile. "And don't worry, I'll be checking in on you."

# SUMMARY

Finding a new box means taking a serious look at your community and how you can change some of the ideas or beliefs that you might currently hold. Many will dismiss these tactics immediately and say they will never work for their business because their business is unique or special. You are correct, your business is unique and special, and this is why you must be willing to look for talent in unconventional ways.

In this chapter, we discussed creating a unique situation that you can apply to your local talent pool with regard to how schedules and job positions are structured. We discussed the pros and cons of stealing employees and what you should consider before doing so. Sharing employees is another great tactic for finding top-level talent and creating win-win situations for you, your business neighbors, and potential employees.

1.  Create a unique situation that works for you and the people in your community.

A. Create new ways to recruit people that are targeted at the demographic in your area.

B. Do you have an abundance of college students or another unique demographic that you can pull from?

C. Can you change the way you structure the job position or schedule to accommodate this pool of talent making your organization more appealing to this demographic?

2. Stealing employees.

A. Stealing employees is an old school trick of the fortune 500.

B. Do you offer something that makes it appealing for someone to jump ship? Maybe it's your 'why they should work for you' from chapter three. Think about what sets you apart or that can set you apart. Is it flexible schedules for better work-life balance or maybe a great leadership program. Perhaps your known for being the best in the business and have a great training program.

C. Use caution when stealing employees. This is often a short-term solution. Stealing employees is often expensive, but it can be a great option if the potential new hire has unique knowledge or skills.

3. Sharing employees.
   A. Great for part-time positions, but can also work for seasonal and full-time positions.
   B. Network with your powerbase to find potential new hires.
   C. Ask your fellow business neighbors if they have any great employees that might want more hours. You will be surprised at how many are willing to share an employee with you that they don't want to lose, but they themselves can't give the employee enough hours.

# CHAPTER EIGHT
## FIGHTING BIG

Even though he had been in Sara's business many times before, Morgan didn't recognize any of the faces behind the counter. He wasn't there to eat but simply wanted to check in and see how his friend was doing. He patiently waited for his turn at the counter then asked the young man, "Is Sara in?"

"Yes, sir and you are lucky you caught her. She was just about to leave," replied the young man. "Who may I say is asking?"

"Tell her it's her old friend Morgan, but I don't want to bother her is she is busy," said Morgan.

"Oh no, sir. She's not mixing batter or anything. She's in her office," the young man said with a smile. "Give me a second and I'll go get her." The young man disappeared for a few minutes then returned saying, "She's in her office, Sir. Just down that hall," He said with a gesture of his thumb. "Do you need me to show you the way?"

"Thank you, but that won't be necessary. I'm sure I can find it," Morgan said with a nod.

As Morgan made his way down the hall, he noticed a picture frame with no photo in it. Where the photo should have been was a piece of plain white paper with the words 'What sets us apart and makes us the 'go-to' place everyone wants to work' printed on it. He smiled a little as he paused to look at it.

Morgan was literally stunned as he walked into Sara's office. She was sitting behind her desk with her hands folded in a relaxed position. She seemed to have a glow about her. Morgan thought she must have looked ten years younger as he stared at her. All the stress and worry that she had in her face just a few months ago was gone.

"Morgan, how are you?" she asked as she came around the desk and gave her friend a hug.

"I'm doing well," replied Morgan. "How are you doing on being small and fighting big?"

"Doing excellent," said Sara. "I'm sure you noticed my print in the hall."

"Yes, I did," said Morgan with a boyish grin. "So, what's the answer, and does everyone on your staff know it?"

"They most certainly do and the answer is to respect one another," Sara said with a smile. "I know it's not fancy, but it's a major shift in our culture and has changed everything for us."

"Really, how so?" Morgan asked with a curious look

on his face.

"Well, and I hate to admit it," Sara said putting her head down for a second before continuing on. "But I wasn't the easiest person to work with, especially before my morning coffee. My attitude affected the attitude of everyone else, for the entire day. I was setting a tone of negativity and disrespect and didn't even realize it. I had a reputation for not being a place where people wanted to work. I had to change that and your lesson on no more excuses snapped me back to reality."

"That's awesome Sara and it takes a lot for us to admit our faults," said Morgan. "I'm very proud of you. So, how are you showing respect?"

"No more yelling and no more screaming to start," said Sara. "If there is a problem, we as a team sort it out. I include the team members on just about everything. Even the small problems. They really appreciate being included and to be honest they often have some really good ideas. I also put out the schedule 2 weeks in advance and try to accommodate them as much as possible. When I can't I always have a conversation with that individual and explain why. No more attitude of me telling them to just suck it up."

"That's really great," said Morgan. "Has it helped with recruiting?"

"Oh yes," Sara said enthusiastically. "I have a constant

stream of people coming in asking if we are hiring. Which is a good problem to have and will help me when I get ready to expand next year. The word is out that we are a great and fun place to work."

"I'm glad to hear," said Morgan. "What about the other aspects of the system? Have they helped you any?"

"Oh yes," said Sara with a nod. "But I have to admit that digging deep and where to dig was a bit of a challenge. I created job descriptions using those methods for every position that I hire for. The work took a little bit, but it has paid off for me big time."

"How so?" asked Morgan even though he was pretty sure he already knew the answer.

"Well, the obvious one is that I'm making better hiring decisions," replied Sara. "Now that I know where to dig and what I'm looking for exactly, making the right decision has become a lot easier. I also know to stay away from making decisions based around the surface layers. I still make a bad hire every now and then, but I go deep and find gold more often than not."

"And that's the whole point, right?" said Morgan. Making more of a statement than asking a question. "Have you been using the structured interview?"

"Oh yes of course," said Sara. "The whole process of digging deep and knowing where to dig would be useless if you didn't apply it with a structured interview. I have created separate interview questions and/or a separate structured interview for each position that I hire for. No more generic and random questions for me. It really has helped me determine if someone has what I'm looking for exactly or not."

"It really is crucial to the entire be small fight, big system," said Morgan waving his finger in the air. "What about finding a new box? Were you able to apply any of those techniques?"

"Actually, I did," said Sara almost giddy. "At first, I dismissed them as useful just as you predicted, but the more I thought about them I got some ideas. The first was what if I changed my prep schedule to the evening before versus in the mornings? Would this help me attract some talent from the local college? I did just that and wow! It opened up the doors to an entire talent pool that I previously had never considered."

Morgan just smiled ear to ear as she went on. "I also share a manager with the salon next door," said Sara. "She just works mornings for me part-time and at the salon in the afternoon. It has taken a huge weight off my shoulders. She even does a little of the bookkeeping for me. She is glad to have the extra hours and it really is a win-win for everyone. I haven't had a need to steal anyone yet, but I'm sure I will once I expand next year and open another location."

"That's great to hear," said Morgan. "I really am glad to see you doing so well and using the be small fight, big system to great effect. Do you have questions for me?"

"Yes, just one," Sara said softly before pausing. "What do I owe you for teaching me the be small-fight big method?"

Morgan smiled, "Only this. Teach others what you have learned about the be small fight, big system. Teach any small business owner or anyone struggling with hiring great talent the process for finding and building better teams. Do that, and we can call it even."

"Deal, I can do that," she said with a smile.

As Morgan made his way to his car, he thought to himself. She most certainly would. She would tell others about the be small-fight big method. It had helped her business tremendously just as it had helped his, and it will help others.

# ABOUT THE AUTHOR

Benjamin Vezina is the founder and CEO of Vezina Consulting, L.L.C. He has owned/operated numerous small businesses in a variety of industries. He has hired people from all walks of life and created numerous high performing teams.

He holds a bachelor's degree in psychology and a master's degree in industrial organizational psychology. He is a certified executive coach and enjoys helping small business owners and their organizations achieve their full potential.

He is also the host of The Next Level Leadership and Small Business Owner Show.

He lives with his wife and two children in South Louisiana.

# SERVICES AVAILABLE

Vezina Consulting is committed to helping small businesses thrive and perform to their fullest potential. The methods and constructs in this book have helped countless organizations build high performing teams and thrive in uncertain market conditions.

If you would like to learn more about how to apply these methods to your organization, or would like to know more about the other products and services offered by Vezina Consulting please contact us at:

Vezinaconsulting.com

Vezina Consulting, L.L.C.

PO Box 454

Rosepine, LA 70659